Men's Pattern Drafting
An Introduction to the Direct Measurement System

By Stanley Hostek

Published and Produced by
Stanley Hostek Tailoring
3213 West Wheeler Street, #187
Seattle, Washington 98199
www.stanleyhostek.com

If you have any questions or comments about this book, please contact:

Stanley Hostek Tailoring
3213 West Wheeler Street, #187
Seattle, Washington 98199
info@stanleyhostek.com

Stanley Hostek
1918-2014

Stanley was born in Lewistown, Montana, where he grew up on his grandfather's horse ranch, learned the tailoring trade from his father, and formed a deep appreciation of his Czechoslovakian heritage.

Stan's upbringing in Montana cultivated his passion for Western and Native American art, literature and movies. He became a resident of Seattle, Washington in 1937 where he met his wife Dorothy. They raised two children and spent 71 years of marriage together,

Stanley was a custom tailor published many times in Threads Magazine. During his career, Stanley owned his own tailoring shop, taught tailoring at Edison Technical School (now Seattle Central Community College) and authored a collection of instructional tailoring books in the 1970's:

Men's Custom Tailored Coats
Men's Custom Tailored Pants
Men's Custom Tailored Vests
Hand Stitches for the Fine Custom Tailored Garment
Men's Pattern Drafting

Even in retirement, Stanley enjoyed teaching others the tailoring trade in the hope of carrying on its old-world legacy and importance.

He was a Past Master of Montlake Masonic Lodge, No. 278, and he served in the European Theater in World War II, storming Utah Beach in the D-Day invasion of Normandy.

Stanley passed his tailoring book business on to his four grandchildren in 2012, so that his work could continue into the future. They formed Stanley Hostek Tailoring and run his website, StanleyHostek.com.

A Note from Stanley Hostek Tailoring

Thank you for your purchase of *Men's Pattern Drafting, An Introduction to the Direct Measurement System*. We hope that the information contained in its pages is valuable to you and your craft.

You will notice that there are a number of pages in this book that are blank with only a page number at the bottom. Please note that this is intentional. Stanley loved tailoring comics and he added quite a few to the original version of the *Men's Pattern Drafting* textbook for his students to enjoy. We have had to remove them due to copyrights, it was done in our efforts to make this book available to the public. Pages were left blank so that page numbers still align with older editions of the book that are in circulations and still used in classes.

We have otherwise left the book in its original form, which you will notice, was written on a typewriter and illustrated by hand. The original was misplaced long ago as Stanley made edits and new copies throughout the years, thus crispness and clarity are lacking. Out of Stanley's five books, this one has had the toughest time making it through the past 40 years or so, but it is still rich with information. We have left it intact to the best of our abilities and we hope that you enjoy.

MEN'S PATTERN DRAFTING
An Introduction to the Direct Measurement System

Stanley Hostek

AN INTRODUCTION TO PATTERN DRAFTING

The conversion of measurements into a pattern is the job of a cutter, sometimes called a designer. His success depends not only on his ability to accurately obtain and apply measurements to the draft (pattern) but to style the resulting garment in such a way as to make it marketable. The cutters' responsibility for "packaging" 7/8ths of the human male form, without ugliness, is huge indeed and not one to be taken lightly.

His principle tool is the division square which is also called a "tailors", "graduated", or "scale" square. It is used to form right angles, measure inches and divide distances.

Measurements may be classified into three groups:
1. LENGTHS   - Those that indicate a vertical length such as waist length, coat length, sleeve length, etc.

2. ROUNDS   - Those that indicate size horizontally such as breast, waist, seat, etc.

3. DIRECT - or also referred to as "SHORT" - These measure-ments indicate attitude (which means posture to a cutter) and are called scye depth, strap, over-shoulder and blade.

"Lengths" and "Rounds" indicate size, "Direct" indicate attitude.

Fabricating (making) or Busheling (altering) garments requires skill in three unrelated areas ie; Hand Sewing, Machine Sewing and Pressing. A pattern is the result of combining two unrelated skills ie; Math and Art.

MATH, or the accurate application of measurements and fractions thereof, is relied on to obtain a pattern that conforms to a persons' size and attitude.

ART, or design has to do with the parts of a pattern that contribute to the attractiveness or saleability of a garment and has no bearing on its physical conformity.

The procedure followed to develop a pattern is referred to as a SYSTEM.

SYSTEMS go by many names but essentially all are based on one of two approaches, either PROPORTIONATE or DIRECT MEASURE.

The PROPORTIONATE approach relies on measurements that indicate LENGTH AND ROUND dimensions whereas the DIRECT MEASURE approach relies on LENGTH, ROUND and DIRECT dimensions. The direct measurements indicate attitude and are peculiar to this approach. To state it another way the use of a proportionate system results in a pattern that will conform to a person with a "normal" attitude and if the persons' attitude is not normal a manipulation (adjustment) must be made in the completed pattern to accommodate the abnormality. A direct measure system incorporates attitude measurements and not only results in a pattern that conforms to size but one that also conforms to attitude and thus requires no manipulation.

Each system has a popular following. The proportionate system results essentially in a BLOCK pattern. "Block" means a previously constructed (and also commercially available) pattern made up in a standard size for a person with a normal attitude and the cutter must be knowledgeable enough to make any change in the pattern to adapt it to a particular customer. A cutter using the proportionate approach then, must be able to analyze his customers' attitude and translate that information to the pattern.

2

The adherents to the direct measure system utilize more measurements (direct measures that indicate attitude) which results in a pattern that is automatically "manipulated" to the customers' attitude. It is obvious that to obtain satisfactory results, using this system, the "direct" measurements must accurately reflect the customers' true attitude. Any slight discrepancy is enough to louse up the whole deal.

What it boils down to then, as a beginner, is the question of whether one wants to develop normal patterns and rely on observation to manipulate them, or train oneself in the art of obtaining direct measurements that accurately reflect attitude. It is not a choice that can be based on relative simplicity as both require much effort and practice. Some cutters combine both by developing a pattern for the body of a coat and rely on blocks for the sleeves for instance. The distinction between the two systems is not so clearly defined by the time a student becomes a skilled pattern maker as he will utilize knowledge essential to both to obtain his results.

Human vanity forces a constant change in style and thus the impossibility of setting down "cut and dried" procedures in pattern development becomes quite obvious. The "math" effort that goes into a pattern remains rather constant but it is the "art" or design aspect of a pattern (which is becoming the dominant factor) that makes it frustrating for a learner due to the lack of something definite to provide him a firmer footing. Serious contemplation of this situation should result in the conclusion that creative challenge is much more desirable than unchanging - regimented procedure even though, for a beginner, it can make the learning process quite painful.

A pattern consists of many parts that must be skillfully blended to form the basis for a marketable garment. The type of pockets, positioning of pockets, darts and their po$1tion1ng, buttons, {number, spacing and positioning), shape and size of lapel, shape of front edge, styling of waist, shoulders and back all must complement one another to the end that the original style objective is acheived.

The challenge to "package" the human body, concealing all its' faults and complementing all its' virtues is compounded by the fact that the mind (of the customer) might have an unconscious, pre-conceived idea of the image its' body wishes to present which becomes apparent only after the garment is completed.

A background in developing patterns is of immeasurable value in fabrication and busheling because it naturally follows that a coat maker has a better understanding of the intended relationships of the parts of a garment if he has such a background and for the bushelman who wants to excel in this area a clear understanding of the pattern that originally produced the garment to be altered is indispensable.

MEASURING THE HUMAN BODY

Accuracy in obtaining the measurements necessary to develop a pattern is obviously important. The difficulty is compounded by the plastic nature of the body and the tendency of the person being measured to "pose".

Most cutters not only rely on measurements but also on observation to confirm those measurements (this is possible by comparing measurements taken with prepared and accepted tables listing proportionate measurements for various sizes). The object of course is to obtain measurements while the person is standing as he normally does. It is quite natural for the person being measured to "go into a brace", pulling in his stomach, expanding his chest and straightening his back. Measurements taken under these conditions, if they do not reflect his normal attitude, are of course useless. The problem then is to create as relaxed a situation as possible when measurements are taken.

Many aids and gimmicks are available in the form of devices that establish measuring points, indicate attitude and even go so far as to involve photography. If they reflect a person's normal attitude fine, if not, they are of dubious value. Psychologically they may have some merit.

A definite sequence of obtaining measurements should be established early in the learning period to make for a more systematic approach, and once established, it reduces the possibility of inadvertently omitting an important measurement. The number of measurements taken is kept to a minimum, therefore each has its special importance.

COAT MEASUREMENTS

WAIST LENGTH, COAT LENGTH, BACK WIDTH, SLEEVE LENGTH - (With coat on)

Before measuring determine the amount of shirt collar the customer wishes exposed above the coat collar (some of the shirt collar should be exposed to protect the coat collar from becoming soiled). The amount exposed will vary from 1/4" to 3/4" depending on the effect desired in the shoulder area. The higher the coat collar, the more "sloped" the shoulders will appear, the lower the collar, the more "squared" the shoulders will appear. If the coat the customer is wearing is satisfactory simply turn up the collar and start the measurement from the seam as shown at "A", Fig. I.

WAIST LENGTH

Measure from "A" to hollow of waist at "B".

COAT LENGTH

Measure to length desired, from "A" to "C".

BACK WIDTH

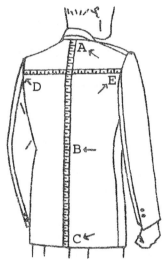

This is a supplementary measurement and is taken to definitely establish the width of the back according to the style desired. Back widths (for the same size) vary, sometimes to extremes, according to style. A large, square shoulder effect would require more width, a natural or "ivy" effect would require less. Fig. I, "D" to "E" shows the measurement taken between the armscyes about 3" below the shoulder.

Fig. I

SLEEVE LENGTH

This measurement is taken on the inseam of the sleeve from the armscye to the desired length. See Fig. II.

A "custom" armscye is usually fitted closer than one mass produced so observe and compensate if the existing armscye isn't properly fitted. The length of the coat sleeve should expose some of the shirt (cuff) as at the neck line (collar) but the average customer prefers a longer sleeve.

Fig. II

SCYE DEPTH, STRAP, OVERSHOULDER, BLADE - (With coat off)

To obtain these "short" measurements, two points must be established on the BREAST LINE. Establish one an inch and a quarter in front of the arm and the other at the center back. It measurements are taken over a vest, and it doesn't fit snug, pin the sides of the vest under the arms to prevent the points to be established from shifting position. If measurements are taken over a shirt, a wide (1" to 1½") band of tape or material should be fitted snug around the breast line and pinned for this same purpose (it will provide a firm base on the breast line to establish the points).

The point in front of the arm will be established by first placing the long arm of the square snug (but not tight) under the right arm as shown, Fig. III. Mark a line with chalk or a pin along the top edge of the square 1-1/4" or so in front of the arm.

Now re-position the square as shown, Fig. IV. Place another mark or pin crossing the first mark, forming a "point" the width of the square (1-1/4") in front of the arm.

Fig. III

Fig. IV

COAT MEASUREMENTS, CONT,

After establishing this point, place a square and a yard and a quarter stick together (Fig. V) and measure the distance from the point to the floor. After the length is determined proceed as shown (Fig. VI), marking the same distance from the floor up on the center of the back.

Fig. V   Fig. VI

SCYE DEPTH
The amount of shirt collar to be exposed having been previously determined, measure down from that point 1-1/4" (width of collar stand) which will be the starting point for the scye depth measurement. Measure straight down the center back to the point established at underarm level, "A" to "B", Fig. VII.

STRAP
Measure from "A", Fig. VII, around the back of the neck, over the shoulder to point "C", Fig. VIII.

OVERSHOULDER
Measure from "B", Fig. VII, over the shoulder to "C", Fig. VIII.

BLADE
Measure from "B", Fig. VII, under the arm to "C", Fig. VIII.

BREAST
Taken from the back around breast (fullest part) at under-arm level not tight - not loose. Fig. IX.

WAIST
Taken from front at natural waist line - easy. Fig. X.

SEAT
Taken from side over fullest part not tight - not loose. Fig. XI.

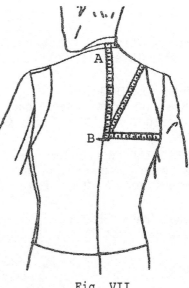

Fig. VII

Fig. VIII

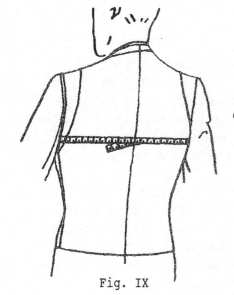

Fig. IX

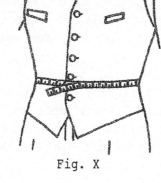

Fig. X

Fig. XI

VEST MEASUREMENTS

In addition to coat measurements (some of which will be used for the vest) take the following measurements:

VEST OPENING
Measure from center back seam "A", Fig. XIII, bring the tape over the shoulder to "B", Fig. XII, actual opening desired.

VEST LENGTH
Measure from center back seam "A", Fig. XIII, bring the tape over the shoulder to "C", Fig. XII, actual lengtb desired.

VEST BACK LENGTH
Measure from "A" to "D", Fig. XIII.

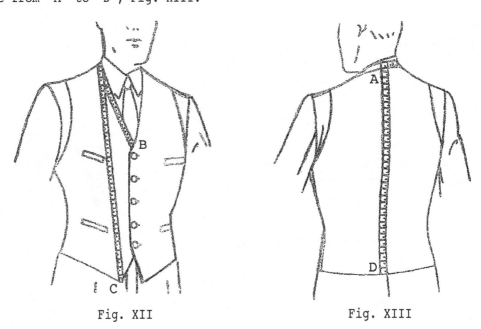

Fig. XII   Fig. XIII

TROUSER MEASUREMENTS

Accuracy in obtaining the outseam and inseam measurements cannot be stressed enough. The primary concern is for an accurate RISE which is reflected in the difference between these two measurements. Difficulty encountered in altering an existing rise is the reason for this. It ls important then that the customer has his trousers adjusted to the desired height at the waistline before the outseam measurement is taken.

The width of the bottom must also be considered in that a trouser leg with a narrow bottom doesn't require the length that one with a wider bottom would. (A wider bottom "clears" more of the shoe). For this reason the approximate size of the trouser leg should be determined prior to measuring in order to know at what level to measure the outseam and inseam.

OUTSEAM
Measure outside of leg from top of waistband to length desired "A" to "B",
Fig. XIV.

INSEAM
Measure inside of leg from snug (not tight) in crotch to length desired
(same level as outseam) "C" to "D", Fig. XIV.

WAIST
Measure around waist at trouser waist-band "A", Fig. XV. Measure over
shirt snug but not tight.

SEAT
Measure around fullest part of seat, not tight - not loose, "B", Fig.
XV.

KNEE AND BOTTOM
Measure between the creases, from the outside, at the knee and bottom level and
double these amounts. See "A" and "B", Fig. XVI.

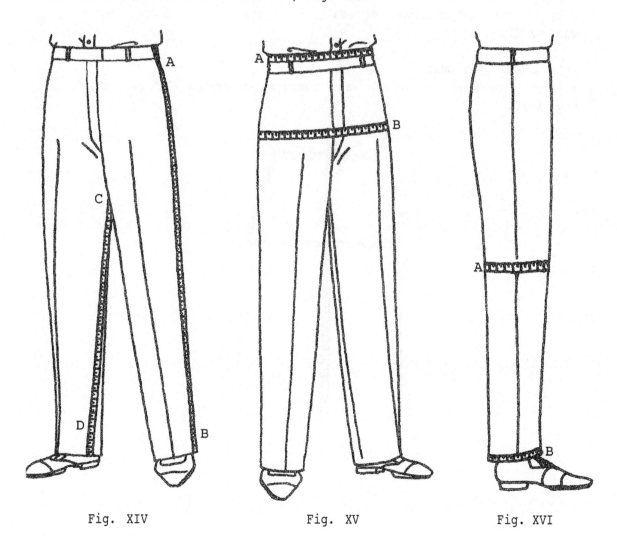

Fig. XIV   Fig. XV   Fig. XVI

Three measurements for the skirt are essential ie; length, waist and seat. Some prefer to augment these with length measurements that not only indicate the front length but also each side and the back. Another suggested measurement is the distance from the waist down to the level the seat measurement is obtained.

LENGTH
Adjust skirt to position desired at waist-line. Measure from top of band to length desired. Note: some measure to the floor and subtract the distance desired from floor to hem, "A" to "B", Fig. XVII.

WAIST
Measure snug over blouse at waist-line, "C", Fig. XVII.

SEAT
Measure over fullest part of seat, not tight - not loose, "D", Fig. XVII.

SEAT LEVEL (OPTIONAL)
Measure from waist to level seat measure was taken, "C" to "D", Fig. XVII.

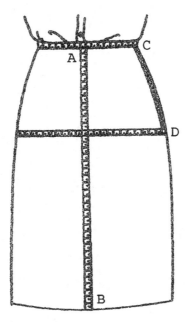

Fig. XVII

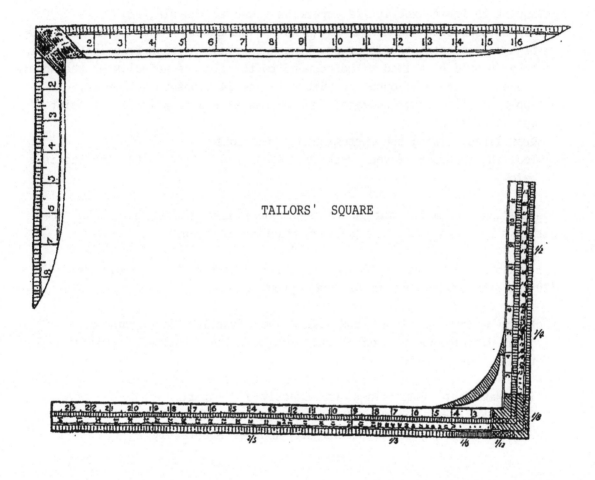

TAILORS' SQUARE

HOW TO MAKE A CHECKER

The purpose of this exercise is to give you practice in measuring distances, squaring lines, and applying the various fractions used on the scale side of the square.

Beside the square, a sharp pencil and an 18" length of drafting paper will be required.

PROCEDURE:

1. Square 25 lines exactly 1/2" apart as shown in the diagram.
2. Number each line starting with number 24 and ending with number 48. These figures represent the lower and higher extremes in each fraction section (they should be halved to correspond to the figures actually on the square place the figure 12 opposite number 24 and 24 opposite number 48.)
3. Apply the fractions indicated from points 24 and 48 using 12 at point 24 and 24 at point 48.
4. Draw lines joining the corresponding fractions.
5. Test ths accuracy of your work by reading and following the instructions below.

The distance from the margin to a diagonal line should be 1/2 of the margin figure in the corresponding fraction section.

For example, from point 40 to the first diagonal line should read "20" in the 1/8th section of the square.

Pick any number at random and check each fraction for accuracy. If your diagram doesn't check out accurately the following points should be re-checked:

1. Make sure your lines are exactly 1/2" apart.
2. Make sure your lines are squared accurately.
3. Make sure your fractions are applied accurately.

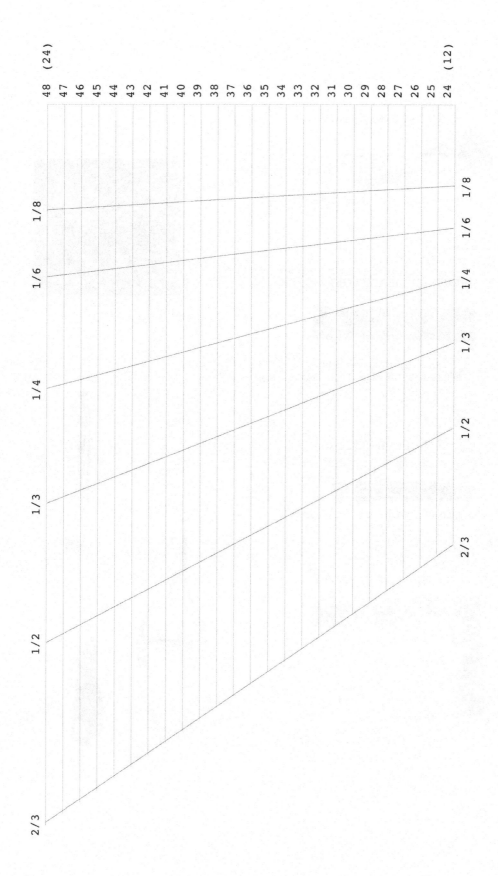

TAPE MEASURE

MADE OF
DOUBLE THICKNESS

LOCK STITCHED EDGE - METAL TIPPED ENDS

BEVELED MEASURING STICK

MADE OF FINE MAPLEWOOD
BRASS CAPPED = 15-INCH LENGTH

CURVE STICK

FINEST QUALITY MAPLEWOOD

BRASS CAPPED - 24-INCH LENGTH
1/8" THICKNESS

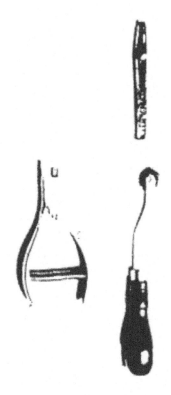

TAILOR'S SQUARE

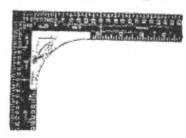

14" X 24"
MADE OF GENUINE BOXWOOD
BRASS CORNER PLATE AND BRACE

PAGE LEFT INTENTIONALLY BLANK

Instructions for drafting the "PANTS, FOREPART" with a French waist.

A is the starting point. Square down and forward.

1 from A = outseam + 3/8"

2 from 1 = inseam

3 from 1 = 1/2 inseam + 2"

4 from 2 = 1/6 seat on division

Add 5" to point 1 for cuff allowance
Drop waist line 2" for French waist
Square out from all points

5 from 2 = 1/3 seat on division

6 from 1 = 1/3 seat on division

Join 5 with 6, locating 7 on line 3

8 from 5 = 1/6 seat on division. Square up, locating 9

10 from 9 = 1/2 waist on division

11 and 12 from 7 are each 1/4 knee measurement. This may be applied by finding the knee measurement in the 1/4 section of the square and placing it on point 7. The angle is marked for point 11 and the knee measurement in the 1/2 section is marked for point 12.

13 and 14 from 6 are each 1/4 bottom measurement.

Shape the outseam as shown. Square up from 10 to line A, curve from 10 to 4, join 4 with 11 and join 11 with a point squared up 2" from 13. Also square down from 13.

Point 15 is where the line from 4 to 11 crosses line 2.

16 from 5 is the same as 15 is from 5

Shape the inseam as shown. Join 16 with 12 and 12 with a point squared up 2" from 14. Also square down from 14. (This will make the inseam and outseam, from 2" above the length through the 5" cuff allowance, parallel with each other.)

Draw a line from a point 1/4" in front of 8 to point 9. This line will be used as a guide to shape the fly. Start at point 9, gradually working away from this line, going through a point about 1/8" in front of this line on line 4, and from there, curve to meet point 16.

PANTS, FOREPART, FRENCH WAIST

MEASUREMENTS

Outseam	41
Inseam	29
Waist	32
Seat	38
Knee	22
Bottom	19

Forward or "out"

Up

Back

Down

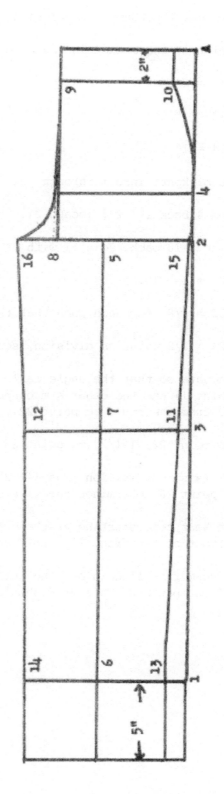

Instructions for drafting the "PANTS, BACKPART" with a French waist.

Cut the forepart pattern out and place it on the remaining paper.

Locate point 17 where the line squared "up" from 8 and "out" from 4, meet.

18 from 16 = 2".

19 from 12 = 1".

20 from 14 = 1".

Shape the backpart inseam through points 20, 19, and 18 as shown.

Sweep from 4 back 1-1/2", locate 21.

Extend line 9-10 back. Join 11 with 21 extending the line to locate point 22.

23 from 22 = 1-1/4".

24 from 23 = 1/8" for each inch that the waist is smaller than the seat.

25 from 24 = 1/2 waist on division, square up.

Fit the square so that the angle falls on the line squared up from 25, with one arm on point 17 and the other arm on point 22, mark both ways (from 17 to the angle and from the angle to point 22). The angle is point 26.

Add 2" to point 22, 1-1/2" to point 26 for the French waist.

Apply 1/2 waist on division plus 1-1/2" from 22 toward 26. The amount between this and point 26 determines the size of dart to be taken out near point 10.

Shape the seat seam starting at the waist line above 26, shape through a point 1/8" in front of the front fly at 17 and about 3/8" above 16 to point 18.

The side seam from 11 down and the cuff are the same for both the back pattern and the front pattern. This area should be traced to complete the backpart.

PANTS, BACKPART, FRENCH WAIST

MEASUREMENTS

Outseam 41
Inseam   29
Waist   32
Seat   38
Knee   22
Bottom   19

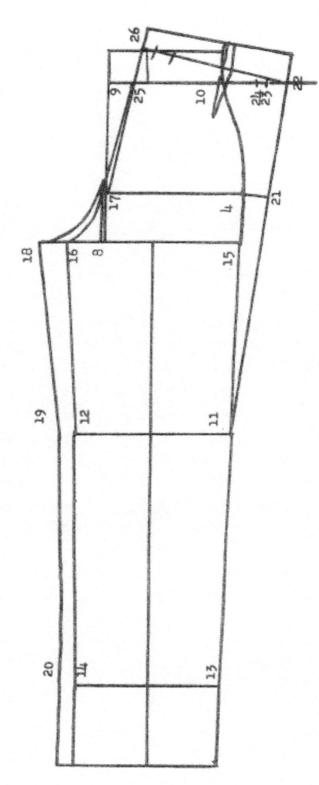

PAGE LEFT INTENTIONALLY BLANK

PAGE LEFT INTENTIONALLY BLANK

INSTRUCTIONS FOR DRAFTING THE PANTS, FOREPART/SEPARATE BAND, PLEATS.

A is the starting point. Square down and forward.

1 from A = outseam minus (width of band desired less 1/4"). Example, 41 outseam minus (1-1/4" band less 1/4" = 1") or 41" - 1" = 40"

2 from 1 = inseam

3 from 1 = 1/2 inseam + 2"

4 from 2 = 1/6 seat on division

Add 5" to point 1 for cuff allowance. Square out from all points.

5 from 2 = 1/3 seat on division.

6 from 1 = 1/3 seat on division.

Join 5 with 6, locating 7 on line 3

8 from 5 = 1/6 seat on division. Square up, locating 9.

10 from 9 = 1/2 waist on division.

B from 10 = 1-1/4" (or allowance for small pleat)

The pattern will eventually be split from the waist line to point 6 and opened at the waist line to provide material for the large pleat. The result of this manipulation increases the size of the knee about 1" so in applying the knee measurement at this time, it is reduced by 1". Example, (22" knee finished, apply 21" knee).

11 and 12 from 7 are each 1/4 (21) knee measurement

13 and 14 from 6 are each 1/4 bottom measurement

Opening the pattern for the large pleat increases the width of the leg at the upper end of the cuff allowance (2" above the length) and decreases the width at the bottom of the cuff allowance (5" below length). The outseam and inseam should be a good 1/4" closer together at the 2" point than 13 is from 14 and a good 1/4" further at the 5" point. This will give the pattern a "bell" effect in this area. The manipulation mentioned for the large pleat will cause the two seams to be parallel with each other through the cuff area.

PANTS, FOREPART, SEPARATE BAND, PLEATS

MEASUREMENTS

Outseam	41
Inseam	29
Waist	32
Seat	38
Knee	22
Bottom	19

Forward or "out"

Up

Down

Back

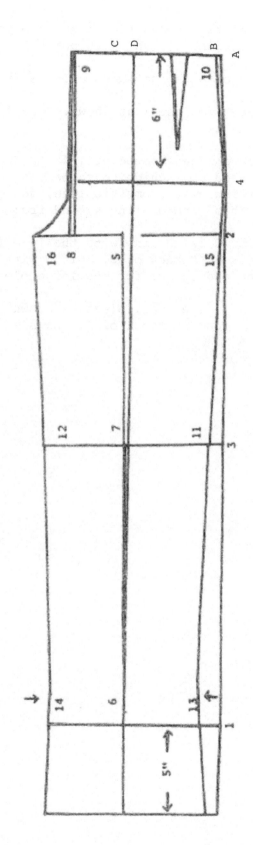

Complete shaping the outseam to point 11 and from 11 to 4, (locating 15 on line 2), and 4 to point B.

16 from 5 is the same as 15 is from 5.

Shape the inseam as shown. Join 16 with 12 and 12 with the point 2″ above 14.

Draw a line from point 1/4″ in front of 8 to point 9. This line will be used as a guide to shape the fly. Starting at point 9, gradually working away from this line, going through a point about 1/8″ in front of this line on line 4, and from there curve to meet point 16.

Point C is in line with the line from 6 to 5 extended. Point D is about 3/4″ back of C. Join D with 6. The pattern will be cut on this line and opened for the large pleat.

Mark in the small pleat as shown, 6″ long, centered between D and a 1/4″ seam in front of B. The size should match the allowance from 10 to B.

PAGE LEFT INTENTIONALLY BLANK

27

Instructions for drafting the PANTS, BACKPART/SEPARATE BAND, PLEATS.

Cut the forepart pattern out and place it on the remaining paper.

Locate point 17 where the line squared "up" from 8 and "out" from 4, meet.

18 from 16 = 2".

19 from 12 = 1".

20 from 14 = 1".

Shape the backpart inseam through points 20, 19, and 18 as shown. The seam through the cuff area at 20 should be parallel with line 5-6.

Sweep from 4 back, 1-1/2", locate 21.

Extend line 9-B back. Join 11 with 21 extending the line to locate point 22.

Make the cuff area through point 13 parallel with line 5-6 and join to point 11 to complete the backpart side seam.

The bottom edge of the backpart pattern is the same as the forepart and should be traced.

23 from 22 = 1-1/4"

24 from 23 = 1/8" for each inch that the waist is smaller than the seat.

25 from 24 = 1/2 waist on division, square up.

Fit the square so that the angle falls on the line squared up from 25, with one arm on point 17 and the other arm on point 22, mark both ways (from 17 to the angle and from the angle to point 22). The angle is point 26.

Apply 1/2 waist on division plus 1-1/2" from 22 toward 26. The amount between this and point 26 determines the size of dart to be taken out about 1-1/4" in front of B. The dart should be about 3-1/2" long.

Shape the seat seam starting at point 26, shape through a point 1/8" in front of the front fly at 17 and about 3/8" above 16 to point 18.

PANTS, BACKPART, SEPARATE BAND, PLEATS

MEASUREMENTS

Outseam   41
Inseam   29
Waist   32
Seat   38
Knee   22
Bottom   19

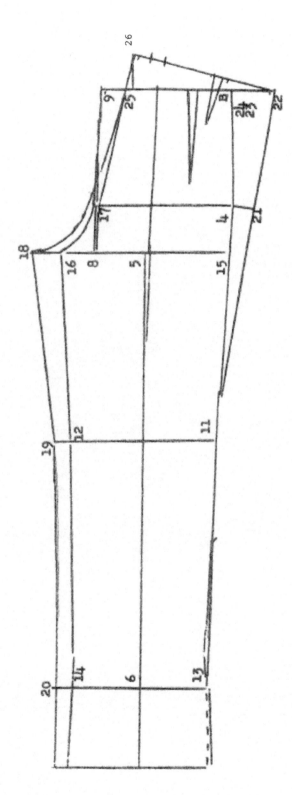

PAGE LEFT INTENTIONALLY BLANK

Table of Proportions
For Short Measure, by Breasts and Heights

HEIGHTS	MEASUREMENTS IN INCHES	33	34	35	36	37	38	39	40	41	42	43	44	45	46	47	48
5'4"	SCYE DEPTH	8 1/8	8 1/4	8 3/8	8 1/2	8 5/8	8 3/4	8 7/8	9	9 1/8	9 1/4	9 3/8	9 1/2	9 5/8	9 3/4	9 7/8	10
	WAIST LENGTH	15 3/4	15 3/4	15 3/4	15 3/4	15 3/4	15 3/4	15 3/4	15 3/4	15 3/4	15 3/4	15 3/4	15 3/4	15 3/4	15 3/4	15 3/4	15 3/4
	STRAP	11 1/8	11 1/4	11 3/8	11 1/2	11 3/4	12	12 1/4	12 1/2	12 3/4	13	13 1/4	13 1/2	13 3/4	14	14 1/4	14 1/2
	OVER SHOULDER	15 3/4	16	16 1/4	16 1/2	16 13/16	17 1/8	17 7/16	17 3/4	18 1/16	18 3/8	18 11/16	19	19 5/16	19 5/8	19 15/16	20 1/4
5'5"	SCYE DEPTH	8 1/4	8 3/8	8 1/2	8 5/8	8 3/4	8 7/8	9	9 1/8	9 1/4	9 3/8	9 1/2	9 5/8	9 3/4	9 7/8	10	10 1/8
	WAIST LENGTH	16	16	16	16	16	16	16	16	16	16	16	16	16	16	16	16
	STRAP	11 1/4	11 3/8	11 1/2	11 5/8	11 7/8	12 1/8	12 3/8	12 5/8	12 7/8	13 1/8	13 3/8	13 5/8	13 7/8	14 1/8	14 3/8	14 5/8
	OVER SHOULDER	15 7/8	16 1/8	16 3/8	16 5/8	16 15/16	17 1/4	17 9/16		18 3/16	18 1/2	18 13/16	19 1/8	19 7/16	19 3/4	20 1/16	20 3/8
5'6"	SCYE DEPTH	8 3/8	8 1/2	8 5/8	8 3/4	8 7/8	9	9 1/8	9 1/4	9 3/8	9 1/2	9 5/8	9 3/4	9 7/8	10	10 1/8	10 1/4
	WAIST LENGTH	16 1/4	16 1/4	16 1/4	16 1/4	16 1/4	16 1/4	16 1/4	16 1/4	16 1/4	16 1/4	16 1/4	16 1/4	16 1/4	16 1/4	16 1/4	16 1/4
	STRAP	11 3/8	11 1/2	11 5/8	11 3/4	12	12 1/4	12 1/2	12 3/4	13	13 1/4	13 1/2	13 3/4	14	14 1/4	14 1/2	14 3/4
	OVER SHOULDER	16	16 1/4	16 1/2	16 3/4	17 1/16	17 3/8	17 11/16	18	18 3/16	18 5/8	18 15/16	19 1/4	19 9/16	19 7/8	20 3/16	20 1/2
5'7"	SCYE DEPTH	8 1/2	8 5/8	8 3/4	8 7/8	9	9 1/8	9 1/4	9 3/8	9 1/2	9 5/8	9 3/4	9 7/8	10	10 1/8	10 1/4	10 3/8
	WAIST LENGTH	16 1/2	16 1/2	16 1/2	16 1/2	16 1/2	16 1/2	16 1/2	16 1/2	16 1/2	16 1/2	16 1/2	16 1/2	16 1/2	16 1/2	16 1/2	16 1/2
	STRAP	11 1/2	11 5/8	11 3/4	11 7/8	12 1/8	12 3/8	12 5/8	12 7/8	13 1/8	13 3/8	13 5/8	13 7/8	14 1/8	14 3/8	14 5/8	14 7/8
	OVER SHOULDER	16 1/8	16 3/8	16 5/8	16 7/8	17 3/16	17 1/2	17 13/16	18 1/8	18 7/16	18 3/4	19 1/16	19 3/8	19 11/16	20	20 5/16	20 5/8
5'8"	SCYE DEPTH	8 5/8	8 3/4	8 7/8	9	9 1/8	9 1/4	9 3/8	9 1/2	9 5/8	9 3/4	9 7/8	10	10 1/8	10 1/4	10 3/8	10 1/2
	WAIST LENGTH	16 3/4	16 3/4	16 3/4	16 3/4	16 3/4	16 3/4	16 3/4	16 3/4	16 3/4	16 3/4	16 3/4	16 3/4	16 3/4	16 3/4	16 3/4	16 3/4
	STRAP	11 5/8	11 3/4	11 7/8	12	12 1/4	12 1/2	12 3/4	13	13 1/4	13 1/2	13 3/4	14	14 1/4	14 1/2	14 3/4	15
	OVER SHOULDER	16 1/4	16 1/2	16 3/4	17	17 5/16	17 5/8	17 15/16	18 1/4	18 9/16	18 7/8	19 3/16	19 1/2	19 13/16	20 1/8	20 7/16	20 3/4
5'9"	SCYE DEPTH	8 3/4	8 7/8	9	9 1/8	9 1/4	9 3/8	9 1/2	9 5/8	9 3/4	9 7/8	10	10 1/8	10 1/4	10 3/8	10 1/2	10 5/8
	WAIST LENGTH	17	17	17	17	17	17	17	17	17	17	17	17	17	17	17	17
	STRAP	11 3/4	11 7/8	12	12 1/8	12 3/8	12 5/8	12 7/8	13 1/8	13 3/8	13 5/8	13 7/8	14 1/8	14 3/8	14 5/8	14 7/8	15 1/8
	OVER SHOULDER	16 3/8	16 5/8	16 7/8	17 1/8	17 7/16	17 3/4	18 1/16	18 3/8	18 11/16	19	19 5/16	19 5/8	19 15/16	20 1/4	20 9/16	20 7/8
5'10"	SCYE DEPTH	8 7/8	9	9 1/8	9 1/4	9 3/8	9 1/2	9 5/8	9 3/4	9 7/8	10	10 1/8	10 1/4	10 3/8	10 1/2	10 5/8	10 3/4
	WAIST LENGTH	17 1/4	17 1/4	17 1/4	17 1/4	17 1/4	17 1/4	17 1/4	17 1/4	17 1/4	17 1/4	17 1/4	17 1/4	17 1/4	17 1/4	17 1/4	17 1/4
	STRAP	11 7/8	12	12 1/8	12 1/4	12 1/2	12 3/4	13	13 1/4	13 1/2	13 3/4	14	14 1/4	14 1/2	14 3/4	15	15 1/4
	OVER SHOULDER	16 1/2	16 3/4	17	17 1/4	17 9/16	17 7/8	18 3/16	18 1/2	18 13/16	19 1/8	19 7/16	19 3/4	20 1/16	20 5/8	20 11/16	21
5'11"	SCYE DEPTH	9	9 1/8	9 1/4	9 3/8	9 1/2	9 5/8	9 3/4	9 7/8	10	10 1/8	10 1/4	10 3/8	10 1/2	10 5/8	10 3/4	10 7/8
	WAIST LENGTH	17 1/2	17 1/2	17 1/2	17 1/2	17 1/2	17 1/2	17 1/2	17 1/2	17 1/2	17 1/2	17 1/2	17 1/2	17 1/2	17 1/2	17 1/2	17 1/2
	STRAP	12	12 1/8	12 1/4	12 3/8	12 5/8	12 7/8	13 1/8	13 3/8	13 5/8	13 7/8	14 1/8	14 3/8	14 5/8	14 7/8	15 1/8	15 3/8
	OVER SHOULDER	16 5/8	16 7/8	17 1/8	17 3/8	17 11/16	18	18 5/16	18 5/8	18 15/16	19 1/4	19 9/16	19 7/8	20 3/16	20 1/2	20 13/16	21 1/8
6'	SCYE DEPTH	9 1/8	9 1/4	9 3/8	9 1/2	9 5/8	9 3/4	9 7/8	10	10 1/8	10 1/4	10 3/8	10 1/2	10 5/8	10 3/4	10 7/8	11
	WAIST LENGTH	17 3/4	17 3/4	17 3/4	17 3/4	17 3/4	17 3/4	17 3/4	17 3/4	17 3/4	17 3/4	17 3/4	17 3/4	17 3/4	17 3/4	17 3/4	17 3/4
	STRAP	12 1/8	12 1/4	12 3/8	12 1/2	12 3/4	13	13 1/4	13 1/2	13 3/4	14	14 1/4	14 1/2	14 3/4	15	15 1/4	15 1/2
	OVER SHOULDER	16 3/4	17	17 1/4	17 1/2	17 13/16	18 1/8	18 7/16	18 3/4	19 1/16	19 3/8	19 11/16	20	20 5/16	20 5/8	20 15/16	21 1/4
BLADE		11 3/4	12	12 1/4	12 1/2	12 3/4	13	13 1/4	13 1/2	13 3/4	14	14 1/4	14 1/2	14 3/4	15	15 1/4	15 1/2

Height - 5'4"

Weight	Breast Meas.	Waist Length	Coat Length	Width of Back	Outside Sleeve	Inside Sleeve	Vest Length	Pants Waist	Pants Seat	Pants Inseam	O'Coat Length
115	34	16	28	7 3/4	29 3/4	16 3/4	24 1/2	28 1/2	36	30 1/4	43
123	35	16	28	7 7/8	29 7/8	16 5/8	24 3/4	30	37	30	43
131	36	16	28	8	30	16 1/2	25	31 1/2	38	29 3/4	43
139	37	16	28	8 1/8	30 1/8	16 3/8	25 1/4	33	39	29 1/2	43
147	38	16	28	8 1/4	30 1/4	16 1/4	25 1/2	34 1/2	40	29 1/4	43
155	39	16	28	8 3/8	30 3/8	16 1/8	25 3/4	36	41	29	43
163	40	16	28	8 1/2	30 1/2	16	26	37 1/2	42	28 3/4	43
171	41	16	28	8 5/8	30 5/8	15 7/8	26 1/4	39	43	28 1/2	43
179	42	16	28	8 3/4	30 3/4	15 3/4	26 1/2	40 1/2	44	28 1/4	43
187	43	16	28	8 7/8	30 7/8	15 5/8	26 3/4	42	45	28	43
195	44	16	28	9	31	15 1/2	27	43 1/2	46	27 3/4	43
203	45	16	28	9 1/8	31 1/8	15 3/8	27 1/4	45	47	27 1/2	43

Height - 5'6"

Weight	Breast Meas.	Waist Length	Coat Length	Width of Back	Outside Sleeve	Inside Sleeve	Vest Length	Pants Waist	Pants Seat	Pants Inseam	O'Coat Length
119	34	16 1/2	29	7 3/4	30 3/4	17 3/4	25	28	36	31 1/2	44 1/2
127	35	16 1/2	29	7 7/8	30 7/8	17 5/8	25 1/4	29 1/2	37	31 1/4	44 1/2
135	36	16 1/2	29	8	31	17 1/2	25 1/2	31	38	31	44 1/2
143	37	16 1/2	29	8 1/8	31 1/8	17 3/8	25 3/4	32 1/2	39	30 3/4	44 1/2
151	38	16 1/2	29	8 1/4	31 1/4	17 1/4	26	34	40	30 1/2	44 1/2
159	39	16 1/2	29	8 3/8	31 3/8	17 1/8	26 1/4	35 1/2	41	30 1/4	44 1/2
167	40	16 1/2	29	8 1/2	31 1/2	17	26 1/2	37	42	30	44 1/2
175	41	16 1/2	29	8 5/8	31 5/8	16 7/8	26 3/4	38 1/2	43	29 3/4	44 1/2
183	42	16 1/2	29	8 3/4	31 3/4	16 3/4	27	40	44	29 1/2	44 1/2
191	43	16 1/2	29	8 7/8	31 7/8	16 5/8	27 1/4	41 1/2	45	29 1/4	44 1/2
199	44	16 1/2	29	9	32	16 1/2	27 1/2	43	46	29	44 1/2
207	45	16 1/2	29	9 1/8	32 1/8	16 3/8	27 3/4	44 1/2	47	28 3/4	44 1/2

Height - 5'8"

Weight	Breast Meas.	Waist Length	Coat Length	Width of Back	Outside Sleeve	Inside Sleeve	Vest Length	Pants Waist	Pants Seat	Pants Inseam	O'Coat Length
123	34	17	30	7 3/4	31 3/4	18 3/4	25 1/2	27 1/2	36	32 3/4	46
131	35	17	30	7 7/8	31 7/8	18 5/8	25 3/4	29	37	32 1/2	46
139	36	17	30	8	32	18 1/2	26	30 1/2	38	32 1/4	46
147	37	17	30	8 1/8	32 1/8	18 3/8	26 1/4	32	39	32	46
155	38	17	30	8 1/4	32 1/4	18 1/4	26 1/2	33 1/2	40	31 3/4	46
163	39	17	30	8 3/8	32 3/8	18 1/8	26 3/4	35	41	31 1/2	46
171	40	17	30	8 1/2	32 1/2	18	27	36 1/2	42	31 1/4	46
179	41	17	30	8 5/8	32 5/8	17 7/8	27 1/4	38	43	31	46
187	42	17	30	8 3/4	32 3/4	17 3/4	27 1/2	39 1/2	44	30 3/4	46
195	43	17	30	8 7/8	32 7/8	17 5/8	27 3/4	41	45	30 1/2	46
203	44	17	30	9	33	17 1/2	28	42 1/2	46	30 1/4	46
211	45	17	30	9 1/8	33 1/8	17 3/8	28 1/4	44	47	30	46

Height - 5'10"

Weight	Breast Meas.	Waist Length	Coat Length	Width of Back	Outside Sleeve	Inside Sleeve	Vest Length	Pants Waist	Pants Seat	Pants Inseam	O'Coat Length
127	34	17 1/2	31	7 3/4	32 3/4	19 3/4	26	27	36	34	47 1/2
135	35	17 1/2	31	7 7/8	32 7/8	19 5/8	26 1/4	28 1/2	37	33 3/4	47 1/2
143	36	17 1/2	31	8	33	19 1/2	26 1/2	30	38	33 1/2	47 1/2
151	37	17 1/2	31	8 1/8	33 1/8	19 3/8	26 3/4	31 1/2	39	33 1/4	47 1/2
159	38	17 1/2	31	8 1/4	33 1/4	19 1/4	27	33	40	33	47 1/2
167	39	17 1/2	31	8 3/8	33 3/8	19 1/8	27 1/4	34 1/2	41	32 3/4	47 1/2
175	40	17 1/2	31	8 1/2	33 1/2	19	27 1/2	36	42	32 1/2	47 1/2
183	41	17 1/2	31	8 5/8	33 5/8	18 7/8	27 3/4	37 1/2	43	32 1/4	47 1/2
191	42	17 1/2	31	8 3/4	33 3/4	18 3/4	28	39	44	32	47 1/2
199	43	17 1/2	31	8 7/8	33 7/8	18 5/8	28 1/4	40 1/2	45	31 3/4	47 1/2
207	44	17 1/2	31	9	34	18 1/2	28 1/2	42	46	31 1/2	47 1/2
215	45	17 1/2	31	9 1/8	34 1/8	18 3/8	28 3/4	43 1/2	47	31 1/4	47 1/2

Height - 6'0"

Weight	Breast Meas.	Waist Length	Coat Length	Width of Back	Outside Sleeve	Inside Sleeve	Vest Length	Pants Waist	Pants Seat	Pants Inseam	O'Coat Length
131	34	18	32	7 3/4	33 3/4	20 3/4	26 1/2	26 1/2	36	35 1/4	49
139	35	18	32	7 7/8	33 7/8	20 5/8	26 3/4	28	37	35	49
147	36	18	32	8	34	20 1/2	27	29 1/2	38	34 3/4	49
155	37	18	32	8 1/8	34 1/8	20 3/8	27 1/4	31	39	34 1/2	49
163	38	18	32	8 1/4	34 1/4	20 1/4	27 1/2	32 1/2	40	34 1/4	49
171	39	18	32	8 3/8	34 3/8	20 1/8	27 3/4	34	41	34	49
179	40	18	32	8 1/2	34 1/2	20	28	35 1/2	42	33 3/4	49
187	41	18	32	8 5/8	34 5/8	19 7/8	28 1/4	37	43	33 1/2	49
195	42	18	32	8 3/4	34 3/4	19 3/4	28 1/2	38 1/2	44	33 1/4	49
203	43	18	32	8 7/8	34 7/8	19 5/8	28 3/4	40	45	33	49
211	44	18	32	9	35	19 1/2	29	41 1/2	46	32 3/4	49
219	45	18	32	9 1/8	35 1/8	19 3/8	29 1/4	43	47	32 1/2	49

Height - 6'2"

Weight	Breast Meas.	Waist Length	Coat Length	Width of Back	Outside Sleeve	Inside Sleeve	Vest Length	Pants Waist	Pants Seat	Pants Inseam	O'Coat Length
135	34	18 1/2	33	7 3/4	34 3/4	21 3/4	27	26	36	36 1/2	50 1/2
143	35	18 1/2	33	7 7/8	34 7/8	21 5/8	27 1/4	27 1/2	37	36 1/4	50 1/2
151	36	18 1/2	33	8	35	21 1/2	27 1/2	29	38	36	50 1/2
159	37	18 1/2	33	8 1/8	35 1/8	21 3/8	27 3/4	30 1/2	39	35 3/4	50 1/2
167	38	18 1/2	33	8 1/4	35 1/4	21 1/4	28	32	40	35 1/2	50 1/2
175	39	18 1/2	33	8 3/8	35 3/8	21 1/8	28 1/4	33 1/2	41	35 1/4	50 1/2
183	40	18 1/2	33	8 1/2	35 1/2	21	28 1/2	35	42	35	50 1/2
191	41	18 1/2	33	8 5/8	35 5/8	20 7/8	28 3/4	36 1/2	43	34 3/4	50 1/2
199	42	18 1/2	33	8 3/4	35 3/4	20 3/4	29	38	44	34 1/2	50 1/2
207	43	18 1/2	33	8 7/8	35 7/8	20 5/8	29 1/4	39 1/2	45	34 1/4	50 1/2
215	44	18 1/2	33	9	36	20 1/2	29 1/2	41	46	34	50 1/2
223	45	18 1/2	33	9 1/8	36 1/8	20 3/8	29 3/4	42 1/2	47	33 3/4	50 1/2

PAGE LEFT INTENTIONALLY BLANK

PAGE LEFT INTENTIONALLY BLANK

Instructions for drafting the COAT, BACKPART.

A is the starting point, square down and forward.

1 from A = scye depth + 1/4".

2 from A = waist length.

3 from 2 = 6" or seat level.

4 from A = full length.

5 is between A and 1.

6 is between A and 5.

Square out from all points.

7 from 2 = 1/2", join 7 with 5, locate 8 on line 1.

9 from 7 = 1/2", join 8 with 9, square from 9 down, locate 10.

11 from 8 = 1/2 blade.

12 from 11 = 1-1/4", square up from 12, locate 13 on line 6.

14 is between 11 and 12.

15 from 10 is the same as 14 from 8.

Join 14 with 15 and square back to 10, 16 is on line 2.

17 from A = 6-1/4", square up.

18 from 17 = 1-3/4", join 18 with A.

19 from A = 1/8" breast on division + 7/8", square up locating 20.

21 from 13 is 1" up and 1/2" out, join 21 with a point 1/4" below 20.

22 from 12 is 1/4 of 12 to 21. Square a short line forward and mark off two 1/4" points.

Shape a curved line from A to 20.

Shape the shoulder seam from point 20, blending it with the straight line about 1/2 way to point 21.

Shape the back armhole by drawing a curved line from point 21 to the first 1/4" point in front of point 22.

Shape the upper part of the side seam from the second 1/4" point in front of point 22 to point 16.

COAT, BACKPART

MEASUREMENTS

Scye Depth	9
Waist Length	17
Full Length	29
Strap	12
Overshoulder	17-1/2
Blade	12-1/2
Breast	36
Waist	32
Seat	38

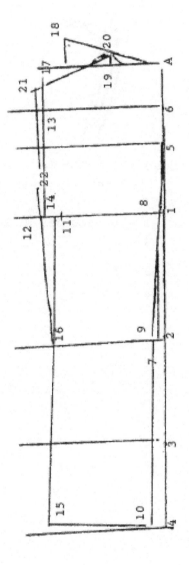

ILLUSTRATION OF SHOULDER WIDTHS

The above sketch shows the difference in shoulder widths of
the same breast side in the different styles.

1 - 1	Shoulder Width	Business Men's Model	Size 40
2 - 2	"	Young Men's Model	"
3 - 3	"	Drape Model	"
4 - 4	"	Extreme Drape	"

Instructions for drafting the COAT, SKELETON FOREPART.

Cut the backpart pattern out and place it on the balance of the paper so that it overlaps enough to include point 47 and so that the original construction lines 1, 2, and 3 form straight lines. Place weights on the backpart pattern to keep it from slipping.

23 from 8 = 1/2 full breast.

24 from 23 = 1-3/4".

25 from 24 = 1/2".

26 is midway between 8 and 23.

27 from 26 = 3-1/2"

Square down from 27, locate 28 on the waist line.

Apply the blade measure from 8 forward and square up. In this case it falls on point 27.

29 from 28 = 1/2 waist on division minus 1/4".

30 is between 28 and 29.

31 is between 27 and 24.

Join 30 with 31 and extend the line up.

32 is located by applying the strap measure plus 3/4" from A to 20 and from 27 to where that amount meets the line extended up from 31.

Join 32 with 5.

33 from 32 is 1/4" to 1/2" less that 21 to 20.

Square forward from 32. 34 from 32 = 1/6 breast on division plus 1/2".
Draw a curved line from 34 to 25.

35 from 34 = 1/6 breast on division.

36 from 32 = 1/8 breast on division minus 1/2". Join to 35 and extend line forward.

37 from 25 = 1".

38 from 29 = 3/4".

Join 37 with 38.

39 from 28 = 3/4" for normal coats, that is where the difference between the breast and waist measure is 4". As this difference becomes greater, increase the distance from 28 to 39 by 1/8" for each inch. As this difference decreases or gets less than 4", reduce that 3/4" by 1/8" for each inch it is less.

Instructions for drafting the COAT, SKELETON FOREPART, CONT.

Example: 37 breast 32 waist, 5" difference. 39 from 28 would be 7/8".
Example: 36 breast 33 waist, 3" difference. 39 from 28 would be 5/8".

Place the angle of the square on 38 with one arm on 39 and square
down. Also join 38 with 39.

40 is on the seat level line.

41 from 38 is the same as 15 from 16.

42 from 41 = 1/8 breast on division minus 1/2", square back a short
distance. (5"-6")

43 from 40 = 3-1/4" (same as 23 to 37).

Points 44 and 45 indicate the edges of the backpart pattern at the
seat level.

Apply the 1/2 full seat measurement from 44 to 45 and from 43 back
locating point 46.

Transfer point 46 to the paper underneath.

Shape the front shoulder seam by dropping 1/4" below point 33 and
curving to about 1/3 of the straight line.

Add another 1/4" point at 22 and shape the armhole as shown.

The backpart side seam is used as a guide to trace the forepart side
seam by turning the backpart pattern over, keep the points at 22 even
and let the lower part of the backpart side seam lay cross point 46.
Trace the side seam. Point 47 is where point 15 falls during tracing.

Shape the hem by drawing a slightly curved line from point 47 to the
line squared back from 42.

COAT, SKELETON FOREPART

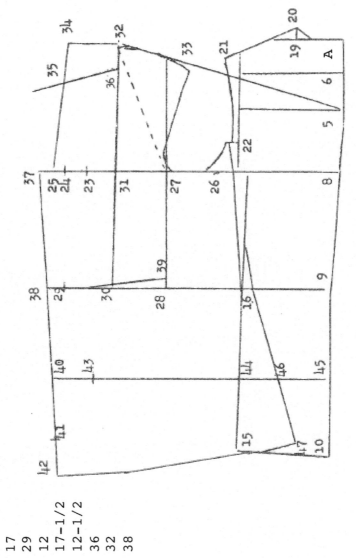

MEASUREMENTS

Scye Depth 9
Waist Length   17
Full Length   29
Strap   12
Overshoulder   17-1/2
Blade   12-1/2
Breast   36
Waist   32
Seat   38

41

PAGE LEFT INTENTIONALLY BLANK

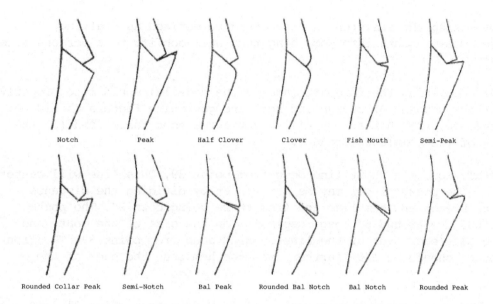

Notch   Peak   Half Clover   Clover   Fish Mouth   Semi-Peak

Rounded Collar Peak   Semi-Notch   Bal Peak   Rounded Bal Notch   Bal Notch   Rounded Peak

COAT, FOREPART, DETAILS

Instructions for adding the details to a skeleton forepart.

These details include the LOWER POCKET, BREAST POCKET, DARTS, BUTTON
PLACEMENT, LAPEL AND FRONT EDGE.

Generally these details have no direct bearing upon the physical conformity
of the garment to the body. It is important however that the appearance of
the finished coat presents a pleasing "picture" to the viewer.

The job of making the skeleton outline could be defined as drafting,
(converting measurements into something that will confirm to a persons size
and shape).

The job of completing the forepart (adding the details) would more properly
come under the heading of design and here the governing factors should be:
(1) convenience, (2) what at the time constitutes good taste, and (3) the
salability of the completed product.

LOWER POCKET: Square a short line down from point 39, This line will center
the pocket. The pocket level may be arrived at by dividing the distance
between the breast and hem line and from there going down 2". The pocket
opening should be around 6" long, depending on the size of the coat, and
divided equally each side of the line squared down from point 39. The front
of the pocket should be 1/8" further from the hem than the back of the
pocket.

BREAST POCKET: Go forward from point 27 1", and down from point 31 3/4". Join
the 1" point to the 3/4" point and make the line (pocket opening) around
4-1/2" long. This may be longer or shorter depending on the size of the coat.
The thickness of the welt is 7/8" and the ends of the welt run vertically.

UNDERARM DART: The underarm dart is a line squared down from the breast line
to a point about 1-1/2" in front of the back opening of the lower pocket.
This may be left as a straight line or shaped out (dash lines) to form waist
suppression.

BREAST DART: The breast dart is placed about 1-1/4" back of the front opening
of the lower pocket. It is parallel with the front edge and around 6" - 7"
long. The size of the dart depends upon the waist suppression and the chest
effect desired. The dart illustrated is strait in the front and hollowed 1/4"
at the center.

COAT, FOREPART, DETAILS, CONT.

BUTTONS: The number of buttons, spacing, and position is left to taste. Form fitted garments should have one of the buttons at the waist line to prevent gapping above or below the fastening. Button location illustrated shows lower button at pocket level, 2nd button 4-1/4″ up.

LAPEL: The crease line of the lapel is drawn from the top button to a point 1-1/4″ in front of point 32. Type, shape and size of lapel varies according to taste. Shape neck gorge by drawing a curved line from point 32, blending it with the strait line 36-35 at a point just inside the crease line.

FRONT EDGE: May be left square or curved to taste. Shape front edge.

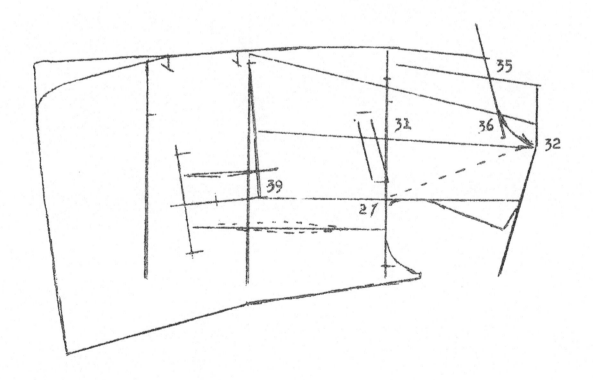

PAGE LEFT INTENTIONALLY BLANK

COAT, FOREPART MANIPULATION

This manipulation tends to reduce the "skirt" and cause the forepart to conform to the body in the hip and waist area.

The forepart patter is cut out. Cut the underarm dart from the armhole to the lower pocket. Cut along lower pocket opening to the breast dart and cut the breast dart.

1. Crease the pattern from "A" to "B".

2. Pleat the pattern over at "B" tapering to "A" enough to open "C" to "D" 3/4". A pin through the pleat will hold it in place. Make sure that the pattern lays flat and that the opening at "C"-"D" remains 3/4".

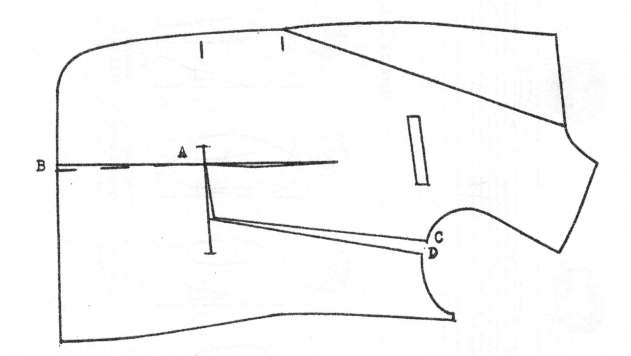

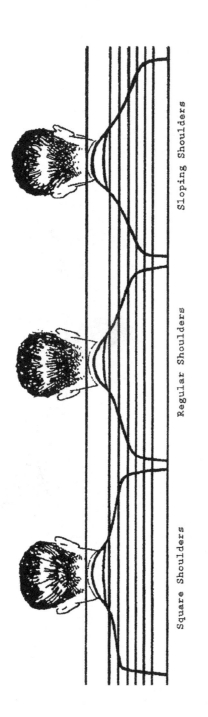

Square Shoulders   Regular Shoulders   Sloping Shoulders

Attitude Description

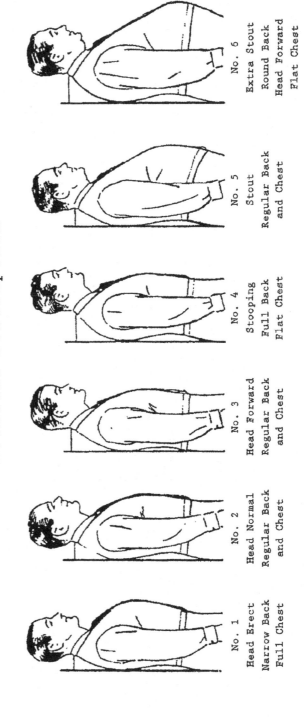

No. 1	No. 2	No. 3	No. 4	No. 5	No. 5
Head Erect	Head Normal	Head Forward	Stooping	Stout	Extra Stout
Narrow Back	Regular Back	Regular Back	Full Back	Regular Back	Round Back
Full Chest	and Chest	and Chest	Flat Chest	and Chest	Head Forward
					Flat Chest

HOW TO MAKE A FACING PATTERN

PARTS: Forepart and paper

TOOLS: Weights, pencil and curve stick

PROCEDURE:
1. Place the forepart pattern on the separate piece of paper to be used
   for the facing pattern in the position indicated in Fig. I. Weight
   pattern down.
2. Point A is where the crease line of the lapel meets the front edge;
   (usually the top button). Trace the front edge from A down and continue
   back along the hemline for about 3-1/2".
3. Measure from the lapel point out 3/4". Remove weights, but do not move
   pattern. Now place the forefinger of your left hand at point A to hold
   the pattern. Pick up the forepart pattern at the shoulder point with
   your right hand and move the upper part of the pattern forward 3/4",
   pivoting at point A. Weight pattern down.

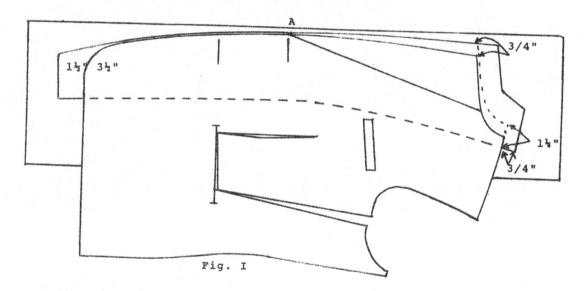

Fig. I

4. Trace the upper part of the pattern from point A to the lapel point,
   continue along neck gorge and back along the shoulder seam for about
   1-1/4".
5. Add 1-1/2" to the length of the facing at the hem, 1-1/2" at the neck
   gorge and 3/4" at the shoulder. Remove pattern.
6. Shape the inside edge of the facing by drawing a curved line from the
   1-1/4" point back of the shoulder point to the 3-1/2" point at the
   hemline. Use the curve stick.
7. Cut out the facing pattern.

49

COAT, UNDERCOLLAR

How to draft an undercollar:

1. Place a piece of paper under the forepart in the collar area. Weight down.

2. Extend the shoulder line and the crease line establishing point 1.

3. 2 from 1 = the same as A to 20 on the backpart.

4. Square down 1/2″ locating 3. Join 3 with 1.

5. Square down from 3, 1-1/4″ locating 4.

6. Square forward from 3, 2″ locating 5.

7. Join 4 with point 32 and trace the neck gorge. Complete as shown.

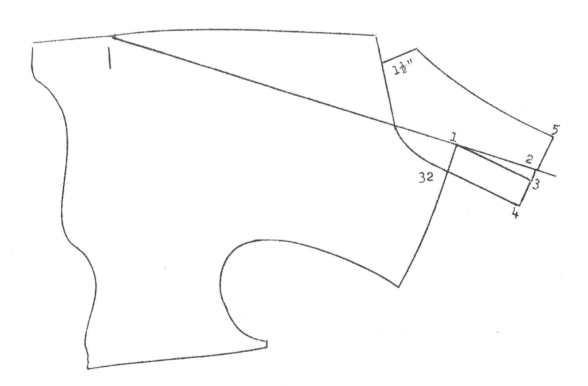

PAGE LEFT INTENTIONALLY BLANK

51

COAT, MEASURING ARMSCYE

Before proceeding with the sleeve pattern, measurements must be obtained from the body of the coat pattern. These measurements are the ARMSCYE, 1/2 ARMSCYE - 1/4", and the SLEEVE DEPTH.

1. Leave the forepart and backpart in the exact position when drafted, Fig. I. Measure the curved line forming the armscye (armhole) from 1 to 2. Follow the dash line at point 22.
2. Locate point 3, (front notch) 1" above the breast line.
3. Now place the pattern so that the shoulder seams butt together and the armscye forms a continuous line. (The neck edge of the shoulder seam will be uneven.) See Fig. II.
4. Locate point 4 by measuring 1/2 armscye minus 1/4" straight across from point 3.

> Example: Armscye = 18-1/2"
> 1/2 armscye - 1/4" = 9"

5. Measure from point 4 to point 5 (original breast line) for the sleeve depth.

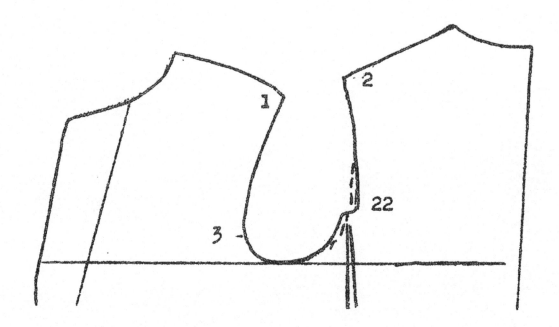

FIG. I

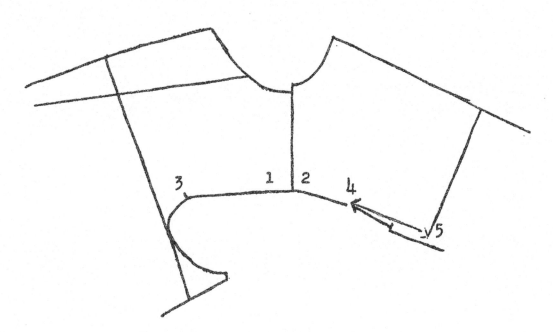

FIG. II

PAGE LEFT INTENTIONALLY BLANK

PAGE LEFT INTENTIONALLY BLANK

COAT, SLEEVE

Instructions for drafting the sleeve pattern.

Starting at point A, square down and back.

1 from A = 1/12 armscye, square back.

2 from 1 = sleeve depth, square back.

3 from 2 = length.

4 from 2 = 1".

5 is between 3 and 4, square back.

6 from 4 = 1/2 armscye minus 1/4", join 6 with 4.

Square down from 6, locate 7 on line 2 and 8 on line 5.

9 from 6 = 16/16" (1").

10 is between 6 and 1.

Square from line 2, locate 11, 12, and 13.

Join 11 with 9.

14 is between A and 13, join with 4.

Place the square with the angle on 3 and the long arm on 12 and square back.

15 from 3 is located by applying 1" more in the 1/2 section on the square
than the hem width desired.
Example: 12" sleeve finished, mark 13 in the 1/2 section.

16 from 2 = 1".

17 from 2 = 7/8".

18 from 5 = 1/4".

19 from 18 = 1-7/8".

20 from 3 = 1".

21 from 3 = 7/8".

COAT, SLEEVE

MEASUREMENTS

Armscye	18-1/2
1/2 Armscye - 1/4"	9
Depth	4-3/4
Length	17

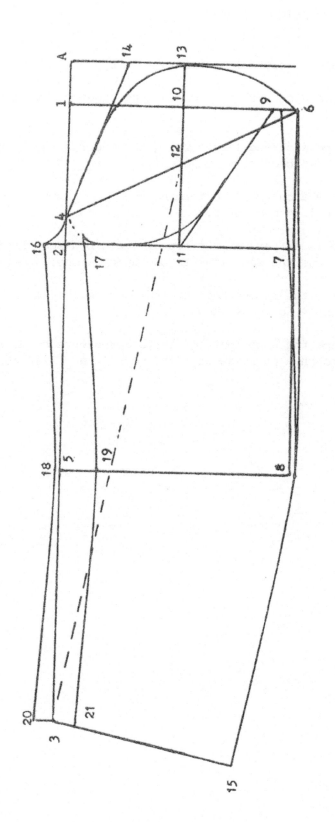

COAT, SLEEVE, CONT.

Shape a curved line forming the top sleeve inseam from 16 through 18 and 20.

Shape a curved line forming the under sleeve inseam from 17 through 19 and 21.

Shape a curved line forming the under sleeve elbow seam from 1/4" back of 9 to 1/4" back of 8 to point 15.

Shape a curved line forming the upper part of the top sleeve elbow seam from 6 to 1/4" back of 8.

The lower part of the top sleeve elbow seam from 1/4" back of 8 down to 15 follows the same line as the under sleeve.

Shape the sleeve head by drawing a curved line from 6 through 13, from 13 to 4 and 4 to 16 as shown.

Shape the upper part of the under sleeve by drawing a curved line from 9 through a point about 1/2" above 11 and 1/4" above 17.

PAGE LEFT INTENTIONALLY BLANK

VEST PATTERN FROM COAT PATTERN

1. Center back seam same as coat.

2. Measure back length from point 1, or make it 3″ below waist line, point A. Draw back length parallel with waist line as shown.

3. Add 1/4″ to the top of the back and the back shoulder as shown, B, C, D. Make back shoulder according to style (3″ to 3-1/2″ average).

4. Drop armscye 1/2 to 1″.

5. Back side seam:

    E from 2 = 1/2 Breast on division plus 1-1/2″.

    F from 3 = 1/2 Waist on division plus 1″.

    Shape back side seam as shown.

6. Forepart side seam: G from 4 = 1-1/2″. Shape as shown, making it 3/8″ shorter at the bottom.

7. Draw line through H, 1/2″ back of line 5-6.

8. I from H = 3/8″ less than back shoulder C-D. Front shoulder of vest is same as coat.

9. J from H = 3/4″.

10. K from H = B-C minus 1/4″.

11. Join J with K, square back 1-1/4″, make stand 1-1/4″.

12. Make front edge of vest 1-1/4″ back of coat edge.

13. L from K = opening plus 1/2″.

14. M from K = length plus 3/4″, form point as desired.

15. Shape bottom of forepart and armscye as shown.

VEST PATTERN FROM COAT PATTERN

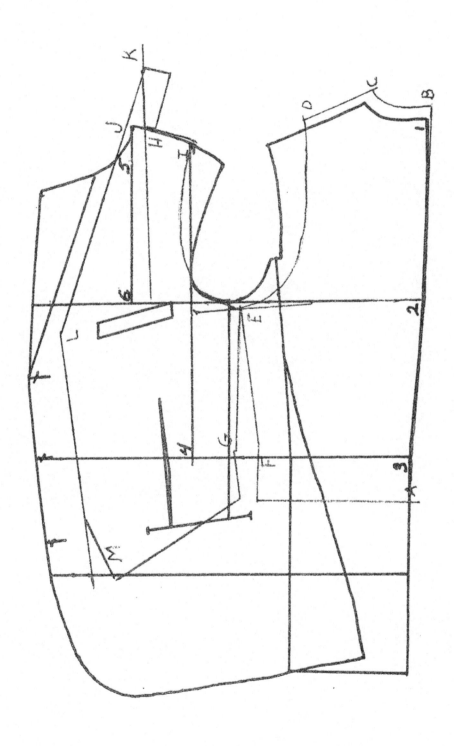

PAGE LEFT INTENTIONALLY BLANK

PAGE LEFT INTENTIONALLY BLANK

INSTRUCTIONS FOR DRAFTING A SKIRT PATTERN

Measurements: Length   27
                   Waist   26
                   Seat   35

0 is the starting point. Square down and forward.

1 from 0 = length plus 1/2".

2 from 0 = seat level, 8".

Square out from 1 and 2.

3 from 2 = 1/2 full seat plus 3/8".

Square up and down from 3 locating 4 and 5.

6 from 2 = 1/2 seat on division.

Square up and down from 6 locating 7 and 8.

9 from 4 = 1/2 full waist. 9 from 0 is the surplus.

10 from 9 = 1/2 of the surplus.

Apply the distance from 9 to 10 equally each side of point 7 locating 11 and 12. Shape from 11 to 6 and 12 to 6. This will reduce the size of the waist at the side seam by an amount equal to 1/2 of the surplus.

Divide 4 to 12 into 3 equal parts locating 13 and 14.

Make 15 from 11 the same as 14 is from 12.

Divide 10 to 0 into 3 equal parts.

Reduce 13, 14, and 15 each 1/3 of 10 to 0 as shown.

16 from 0 = 1/2". Join 16 with 11.

SKIRT DRAFT

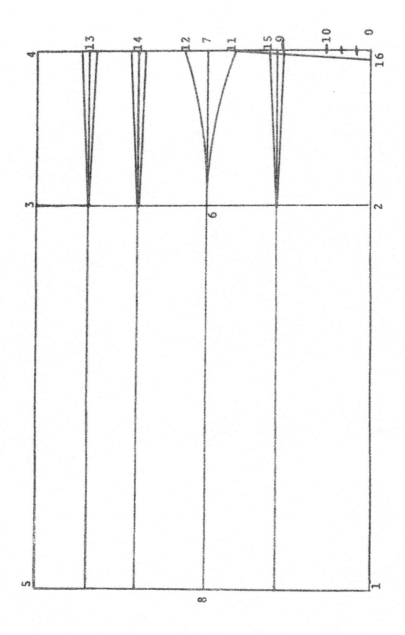

Made in the USA
Monee, IL
16 September 2023